AF599314

SEE IT GROW!
See a Coconut Grow
by Kirsten Chang
BLASTOFF! READERS
1
BELLWETHER MEDIA • MINNEAPOLIS, MN

Blastoff! Readers are carefully developed by literacy experts to build reading stamina and move students toward fluency by combining standards-based content with developmentally appropriate text.

Level 1 provides the most support through repetition of high-frequency words, light text, predictable sentence patterns, and strong visual support.

Level 2 offers early readers a bit more challenge through varied sentences, increased text load, and text-supportive special features.

Level 3 advances early-fluent readers toward fluency through increased text load, less reliance on photos, advancing concepts, longer sentences, and more complex special features.

★ **Blastoff! Universe**

Reading Level

Grade K

Grades 1–3

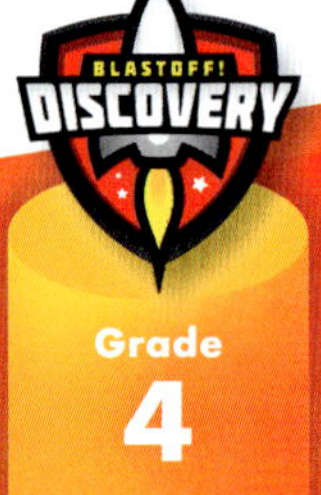

Grade 4

This edition first published in 2024 by Bellwether Media, Inc.

No part of this publication may be reproduced in whole or in part without written permission of the publisher. For information regarding permission, write to Bellwether Media, Inc., Attention: Permissions Department, 6012 Blue Circle Drive, Minnetonka, MN 55343.

Library of Congress Cataloging-in-Publication Data

LC record for See a Coconut Grow available at: https://lccn.loc.gov/2023039899

Text copyright © 2024 by Bellwether Media, Inc. BLASTOFF! READERS and associated logos are trademarks and/or registered trademarks of Bellwether Media, Inc.

Editor: Rachael Barnes Designer: Brittany McIntosh

Printed in the United States of America, North Mankato, MN.

Table of Contents

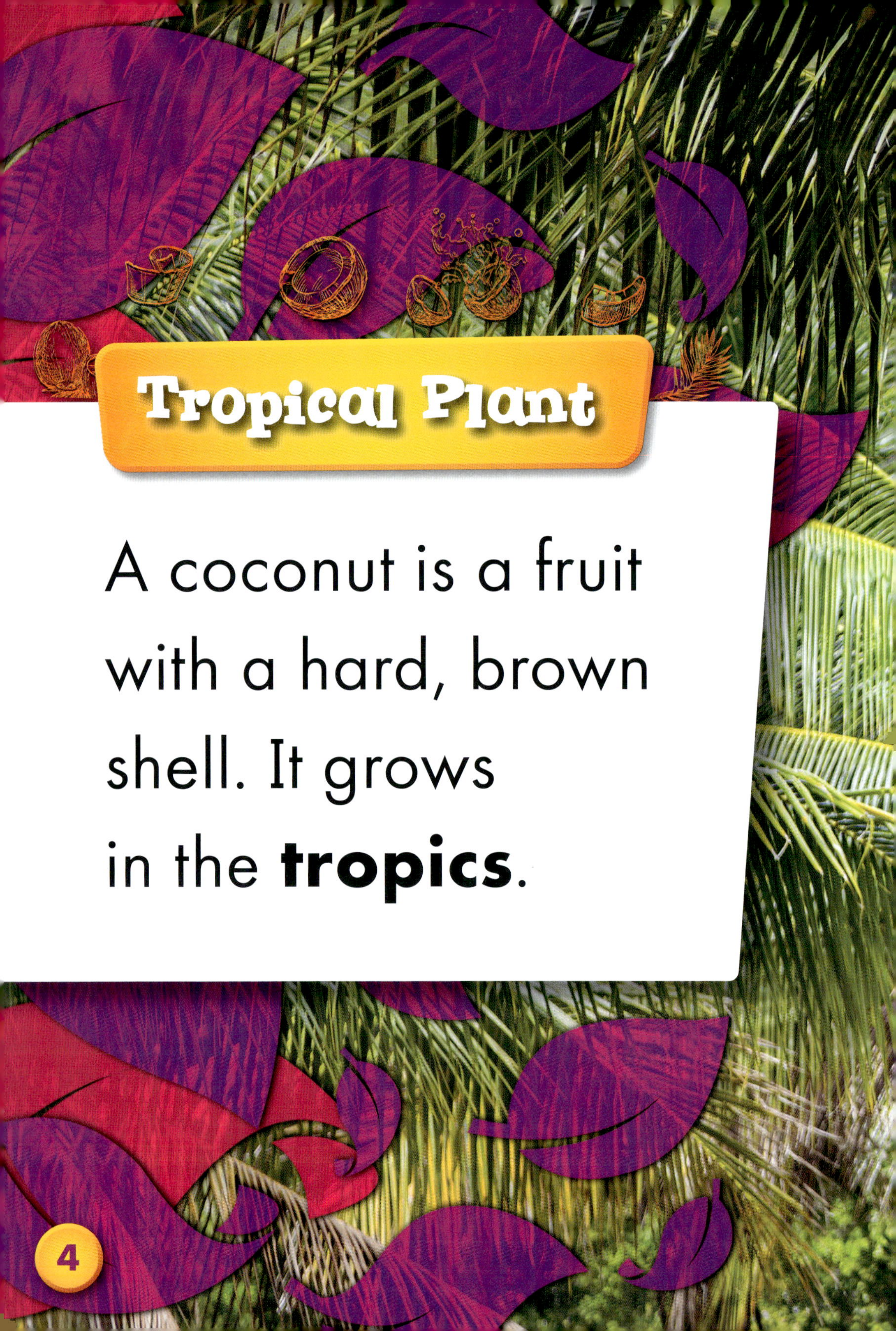

Tropical Plant

A coconut is a fruit with a hard, brown shell. It grows in the **tropics**.

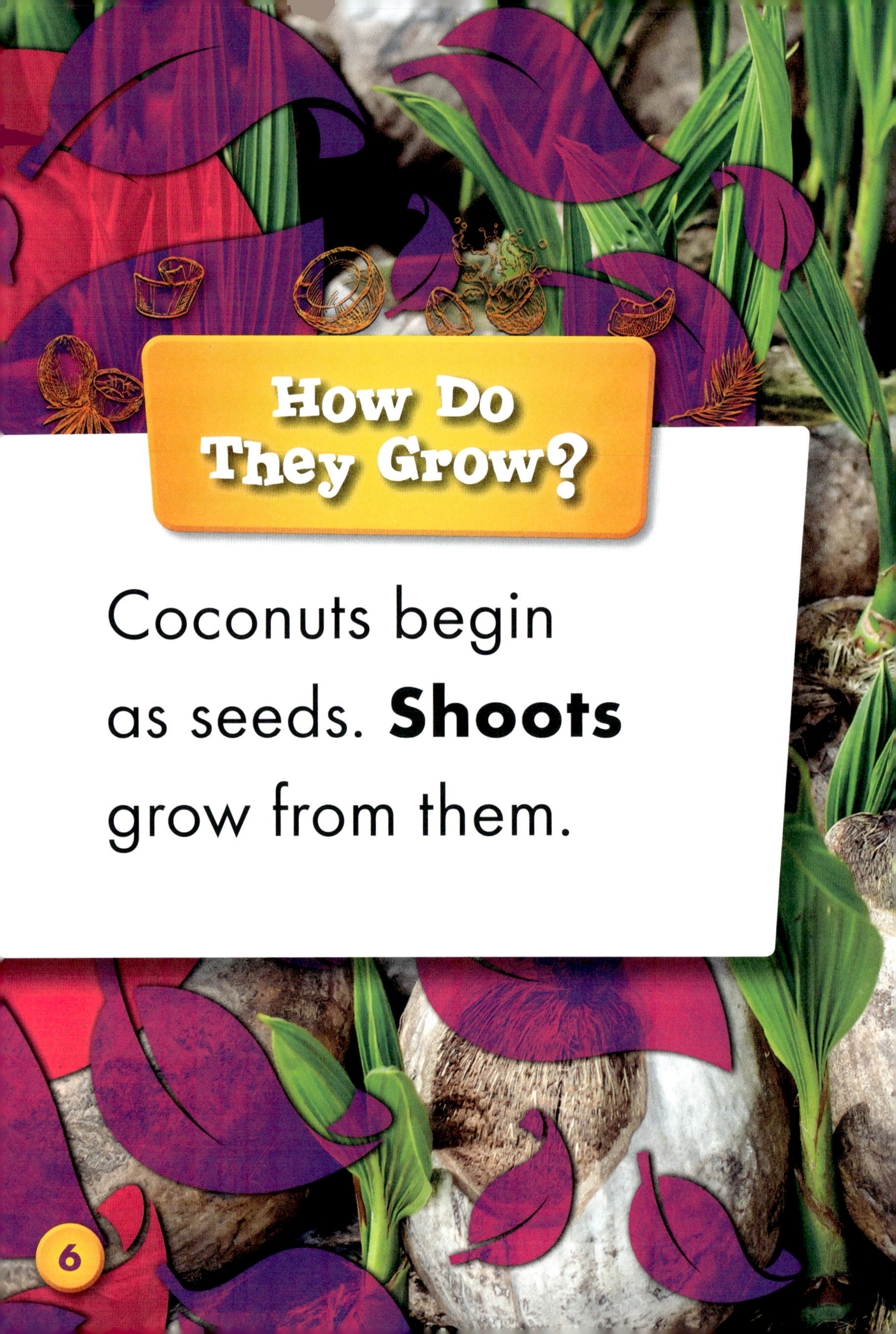

How Do They Grow?

Coconuts begin as seeds. **Shoots** grow from them.

shoot
seed

Shoots need water, sun, and sandy soil. Each shoot grows into a coconut **palm**.

coconut
palm
Needed to Grow
water
sun
sandy
soil

The palm grows a tall trunk and green leaves.

leaves
trunk

After many years, flowers grow at the top of the trunk. Bees **pollinate** the flowers.

flowers
bees pollinating flowers

Coconuts grow from the flowers. Each coconut has an outer skin and **husk**.

husk
skin

Coconuts turn brown as they **ripen**. A hard shell forms around the fruit.

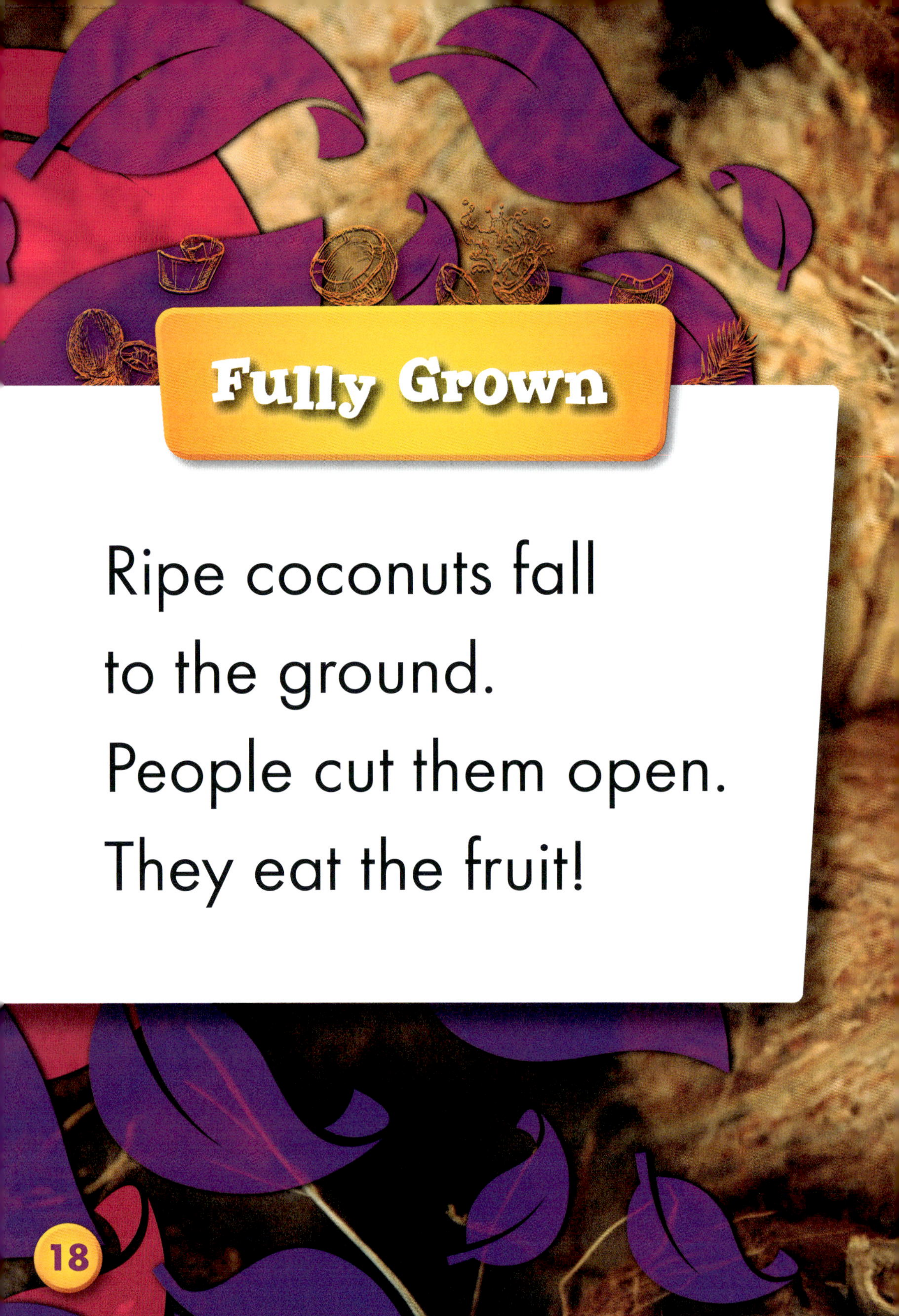

Fully Grown

Ripe coconuts fall to the ground. People cut them open. They eat the fruit!

Using Coconuts
coconut flakes
coconut oil
coconut milk
fruit

Coconuts left
on the ground
grow new palms!

Coconut Life Cycle
1
palm grows
2
flowers grow
3
coconuts grow
4
ripe coconuts fall off

Glossary

husk

the rough outer shell of a coconut

ripen

to become ready to eat

palm

a tropical plant with a tall trunk and large green leaves

shoots

parts of new plants that grow above the ground

pollinate

to give a dust called pollen to make seeds grow

tropics

hot parts of the world

To Learn More

AT THE LIBRARY

Barnham, Kay. *The Amazing Life Cycle of Plants*. Hauppage, N.Y.: Barron's, 2018.

Chang, Kirsten. *See A Pineapple Grow*. Minneapolis, Minn.: Bellwether Media, 2024.

Lee, Jackie. *Coconut*. New York, N.Y.: Bearport Publishing Company, 2016.

ON THE WEB

FACTSURFER

Factsurfer.com gives you a safe, fun way to find more information.

1. Go to www.factsurfer.com.
2. Enter "see a coconut grow" into the search box and click 🔍.
3. Select your book cover to see a list of related content.

Index

The images in this book are reproduced through the courtesy of: Ewa Studio, front cover (coconut); jakkapan, front cover (seedling); wiangya, front cover (shoot); Yeti studio, p. 3; Holger Kleine/ Alamy; pp. 4-5; pittaya, pp. 6-7; Zoonar GmbH/ Alamy, pp. 8-9; Tonio_75, p. 9 (water); cobalt88, p. 9 (sun); art nick, p. 9 (sandy soil); Pretoperola, pp. 10-11; atk work, pp. 12-13; koonsiri boonnak, p. 13 (inset); Pavel Muravev/ Alamy, pp. 14-15; Baramyou0708, p. 15 (inset); TamuT, pp. 16-17; Rahul D Silva, pp. 18-19; New Africa, p. 19 (coconut flakes); Photoongraphy, 19 (coconut oil); Alex Tarassov, p. 19 (coconut milk); Vasiliy Koval, pp. 20-21; Noppamart Wittayapanyanon, p. 22 (husk); trendobjects, p. 22 (palm); taffpixture, p. 22 (pollinate); Cindy Jay Dunn, p. 22 (ripen); Indra saputra iputu, p. 22 (shoots); Altug Galip, p. 22 (tropics); yothinpi, p. 23.